TRUE STORY OF CHRISTMAS

GLAD TIDINGS

TAYO LEO

All Scripture quotations are taken from the King James Version of the Holy Bible.

DEDICATION

This book is dedicated to the Lord Jesus the Reigning King!

True Story of Christmas

Table of Content

INTRODUCTION

The story of Christmas is centered on the birth of a new born King with the appearance of His Star, the wise men, Herod the then King of Judah and the glad tidings declared by the angels to the shepherd.

The new born King is King eternal who reigns from everlasting to everlasting having one of His names as the Everlasting Father. So He was more than a child at birth, He is King Jesus! The appearances of the glory of His Star that shines so bright gave signal that an eternal King is born on earth.

Wise men (the Magi) came from afar to identify with Him who is born King. They came in awe of Him and to worship Him with significant gifts which symbolizes His Royalty, His Divinity and His Humanity.

However at the birth of the new born King, Herod the then King of Judah was bothered and troubled, and wanted the new born King dead, but the new born King survived the conspiracy.

The birth of the new born King brought glad tidings of joy to the world that a saviour is born to reconcile humanity with God. So His birth brought about celebration and declaration by the angels and heavenly host that the Saviour of the world is born.

> *And the angel said unto them, Fear not: for, behold, I bring you good tidings of great joy, which shall be to all people. For unto you is born this day in the city of David a Saviour, which is Christ the Lord.*
> *Luke 2:10-11.*

Chapter one

HE THAT IS BORN A KING!

Now when Jesus was born in Bethlehem of Judaea in the days of Herod the king, behold, there came wise men from the east to Jerusalem, Saying, Where is he that is born King of the Jews? For we have seen his star in the east, and are come to worship him.
Matt. 2:1-2.

Have you met anyone who is born a king: someone who already at his birth is a king? I suggest not, because kings are not born as king but they are coronate or installed as one at some point in their lifetime. But the Lord Jesus is the only One born a reigning King.

According to the above scripture, when the wise men got to the palace their question was; "*Where is He that is born King?"* There have never been anyone born a king; they saw the glory of His star which indicated that He who was born is a reigning King. In their entire journey as wise men they had never seen anyone born a king, so they came to see who He is and to worship Him.

How is He a Reigning King?

He's a reigning King because according to prophecy He's the One of whom the government (kingship, authority) will be upon His shoulder, the expected Messiah.

> *For unto us a child is born, unto us a son is given: and the government shall be upon his shoulder: and his name shall be called Wonderful, Counselor, The mighty God, The everlasting Father, The Prince of Peace. Of the increase of his government and peace there shall be no end, upon the throne of David, and upon his kingdom, to order it, and to establish it with judgment and with justice from henceforth even forever. The zeal of the LORD of hosts will perform this.*
>
> *Isaiah 9:6.*

Also by the prophecy of His virgin birth, He is Immanuel: The God (King) who is with us. "*Therefore the Lord himself shall give you a sign; Behold, a virgin shall conceive, and bear a son, and shall call his name Immanuel"* (Isaiah 7:14). So from birth He's to reign as Wonderful Counselor, The Mighty God, The Everlasting Father, and The Prince of Peace!

The Eternal King

> *But thou, Bethlehem Ephratah, though thou be little among the thousands of Judah, yet out of thee shall he come forth unto me that is to be ruler in Israel; whose goings forth have been from of old, from everlasting. Micah 5:2.*

He has to reign from birth because He reigns from everlasting to everlasting as King eternal, "*Now unto the King eternal, immortal, invisible, the only wise God, be honour and glory for ever and ever. Amen."* (1 Tim. 1:17). He is King in heaven and on earth; He's the King of Glory!

> *Lift up your heads, O ye gates; and be ye lift up, ye everlasting doors; and the King of glory shall come in. Who is this King of glory? The LORD strong and mighty, the LORD mighty in battle. Lift up your heads,*

O ye gates; even lift them up, ye everlasting doors; and the King of glory shall come in. Who is this King of glory? The LORD of hosts, he is the King of glory.
Psalm 24:7-10.

The Declaration!

As King eternal who reigns over heaven and earth, at His birth there was a declaration from heaven by the angels and a confirmation on earth by the wise men that a King is born! So His birth could not happen unaware, unannounced without being noticed both in heaven and on earth.

And so it was, that, while they were there, the days were accomplished that she should be delivered. And she brought forth her firstborn son, and wrapped him in swaddling clothes, and laid him in a manger; because there was no room for them in the inn. And there were in the same country shepherds abiding in the field, keeping watch over their flock by night. And, lo, the angel of the Lord came upon them, and the glory of the Lord shone round about them: and they were sore afraid. And the angel said unto them, Fear

not: for, behold, I bring you good tidings of great joy, which shall be to all people. For unto you is born this day in the city of David a Saviour, which is Christ the Lord. And this shall be a sign unto you; Ye shall find the babe wrapped in swaddling clothes, lying in a manger. And suddenly there was with the angel a multitude of the heavenly host praising God, and saying, Glory to God in the highest, and on earth peace, good will toward men. And it came to pass, as the angels were gone away from them into heaven, the shepherds said one to another, Let us now go even unto Bethlehem, and see this thing which is come to pass, which the Lord hath made known unto us.
Luke 2:6-15.
Now when Jesus was born in Bethlehem of Judaea in the days of Herod the king, behold, there came wise men from the east to Jerusalem, Saying, Where is he that is born King of the Jews? for we have seen his star in the east, and are come to worship him.
Matt. 2:1-2.

According to the scripture in the mouth of two or three witnesses a matter is established, so heavenly host with angels had to declare from heaven, and wise men on earth gave confirmation that a reigning King is born indeed! At His birth therefore, He's not a baby, but King Jesus! So Angels celebrated Him, and the Wise Men bow down to worship Him because He is a born King and live King forever!

> *And when they were come into the house, they saw the young child with Mary his mother, and fell down, and worshipped him: and when they had opened their treasures, they presented unto him gifts; gold, and frankincense, and myrrh.*
>
> *Matt. 2:11.*

Chapter Two

THE WISE MEN

Now when Jesus was born in Bethlehem of Judaea in the days of Herod the king, behold, there came wise men from the east to Jerusalem.
Matt. 2:1.

Who are the Wise Men?

The Magi are magicians. Wise men of old are mysterious people of magic and sorcery with extra ordinary power of manipulation. They are star gazers and star manipulators. In the Bible days those who are refer to as wise men are not common people, as we see in the land of Egypt and in Babylon:

Then Pharaoh also called the wise men and the sorcerers: now the magicians of Egypt, they also did in like manner with their enchantments. For they cast down every man his rod, and they became serpents: but Aaron's rod swallowed up their rods.
Exo. 7:11-12.

Then the king commanded to call the magicians, and the astrologers, and the sorcerers, and the Chaldeans, for to shew the king his dreams. So they came and stood before the king.
Dan. 2:2.
The king cried aloud to bring in the astrologers, the Chaldeans, and the soothsayers. And the king spake, and said to the wise men of Babylon, Whosoever shall read this writing, and shew me the interpretation thereof, shall be clothed with scarlet, and {have} a chain of gold about his neck, and shall be the third ruler in the kingdom. Then came in all the king's wise men: but they could not read the writing, nor make known to the king the interpretation thereof.
Dan. 5:7-8.

The wise men are also philosophers; men which have understanding of times and seasons.

The Glory of the Star

At the birth of the Eternal King was the appearance of the glorious Star that shines so bright which captured the attention of the wise men: A star like no other. The Star was so unique that it shines during the day to give direction to the wise men, because He who is born King is the Bright Morning Star! (Rev. 22:16).

The wise men for who they are can manipulate stars, they can high jack the glory of one star and exchange it for another, but when they saw the glory of the star of the born King they couldn't do anything against it, it was a powerful star that cannot be enchanted, so they had to summit to the Star and identify with it. By divination they were able to discern from the glory of the Star that He who is born is a reigning King.

They made up their mind to cooperate with the star: so as to go see who the King is and to pay homage to Him. So long as they cooperate in submission to the Star, they were led by the Star to Jerusalem.

A Humble King!

Where else could a reigning king be born if not at the palace in Jerusalem: the City of the King! So the wise men having got to Jerusalem headed to the palace in eagerness to see He who is born King!

> *...Behold there came wise men from the east to Jerusalem, Saying, Where is he that is born King of the Jews? for we have seen his star in the east, and are come to worship him.*
> *Matt. 2:1-2.*

The wise men by their speculation were not wrong visiting the palace at first. But because He's a humble King, He came humble at His birth from the least town of Bethlehem after that Joseph and Mary had to go through the valley and the hills from Galilee to Bethlehem by the decree from Caesar Augustus, that all the world should be taxed: which was done in order for the prophecy concerning His birth to be fulfilled.

> *And they said unto him, In Bethlehem of Judaea: for thus it is written by the prophet, And thou Bethlehem, in the land of Juda, art not the least among the princes of Juda: for out of thee shall come a Governor, that shall rule my people Israel.*

> *Matt. 2:5-6.*
>
> *And Joseph also went up from Galilee, out of the city of Nazareth, into Judaea, unto the city of David, which is called Bethlehem; (because he was of the house and lineage of David:) To be taxed with Mary his espoused wife, being great with child. And so it was, that, while they were there, the days were accomplished that she should be delivered. And she brought forth her firstborn son, and wrapped him in swaddling clothes, and laid him in a manger; because there was no room for them in the inn.*
>
> *Luk. 2:4-7.*

He was not found in the palace, so the wise men left the palace in continuous search of the born King as they again followed the star to where the King was born. An Eternal King; but yet a Humble King who was found laid in the manger. What a King!

> *...They departed; and, lo, the star, which they saw in the east, went before them, till it came and stood over where the young child was. When they saw the star, they rejoiced with exceeding great joy. And when they*

were come into the house, they saw the young child with Mary his mother, and fell down, and worshipped him: and when they had opened their treasures, they presented unto him gifts; gold, and frankincense, and myrrh.

Matt. 2:9-11.

The King of Kings

They met the King of kings and the Lord of lords, the Ancient of days, the Bright Morning Star, the Everlasting Father, and they fell down and worshipped Him. For the wise men to fall down and worship they saw more than a child born, He's a King!

By their discernment of the Star the wise men knew already who they have come to seek, so they came prepared with significant gifts to give expression of who the King is.

The Gifts and Significance

The presentation of gifts by the wise men to King Jesus at birth was beyond the immediate scene, it gives the significance of whom He is that is born King. "*And when they had opened their treasures, they presented unto him gifts; gold, and frankincense, and myrrh*" (Matt. 2:11).

Since the Magi are wise men, they presented the gifts connotatively that it takes only the wise to understand the significant of what they did. The gifts of the wise men therefore speak volume than what the wise men could say, so they allow the significance of the gifts to speak of who the born King is: A King, An Immortal Being and A Mortal Being at the same time.

Gold:

Gold in the days of old are gifts presented or offered to kings alone in reverence to their office of Royalty. It symbolizes Kingship.

Frankincense:

Frank-incense which is a kind of incense, is an obligation offered to Spirit Being: as to God as a form of worship. It symbolizes Divinity.

Myrrh:

Myrrh is an ointment use for embalmment of mortal beings. It symbolizes Humanity: human nature.

Therefore, the three gifts presented by the wise men to the Eternal King at His birth on earth signifies His Royalty, His Divinity and His Humanity. So the wise men offered worship, and acknowledged that He didn't come as a Mortal Being alone, but He is Immortal and King Eternal.

> *Now unto the King eternal, immortal, invisible, the only wise God, be honour and glory for ever and ever Amen.*
>
> *1Tim 1:17.*

The Fulfillment

The wise men were fulfilled in their journey, they came from the Far East to worship and to honour Him that is born King. They rejoice with exceeding joy as the Star led them to where the King was born, they were glad when they saw the born King, their mission was accomplished.

On their return they were guided and given direction by the Lord to their destination: which signified that their worship of the born King was accepted, so they were fulfilled and full of joy!

> *And being warned of God in a dream that they should not return to Herod, they departed into their own country another way.*
> *Matt. 2:12.*

Chapter Three

THE CONSPIRACY

There was a conspiracy at the birth of the new born King conspired by Herod the then king of Judah, because he could not imagine how a reigning king would emerge while he (Herod) was yet alive as a king.

> *When Herod the king had heard these things, he was troubled, and all Jerusalem with him. And when he had gathered all the chief priests and scribes of the people together, he demanded of them where Christ should be born. And they said unto him, In Bethlehem of Judaea: for thus it is written by the prophet,*
>
> *Then Herod, when he had privily called the wise men, enquired of them diligently what time the star appeared. And he sent them to Bethlehem, and said, Go and search diligently for the young child; and when ye have found {him}, bring me word again, that I may come and worship him also.*
>
> *Matt. 2:3-5, 7-8.*

Moreover because kings are coronate into office and not born as a reigning king, it became more worrisome for Herod to get rid of the born King so as for him and his lineage not to the dethroned for the born King to be enthroned in his stead.

The birth of the born King became a threat to Herod, unknown to Herod that He was not born to take over the throne from him, but was born to be identified with as King eternal who came as Saviour of the world.

> *And she shall bring forth a son, and thou shalt call his name JESUS: for he shall save his people from their sins.*
> *Matt. 1:21.*
> *And the angel said unto them, Fear not: for, behold, I bring you good tidings of great joy, which shall be to all people. For unto you is born this day in the city of David a Saviour, which is Christ the Lord.*
> *Luke 2:10-11.*

Furthermore; because Herod felt insecure about the birth of the new born King, he plotted for the new born King to be killed.

> *And being warned of God in a dream that they (wise men) should not return to Herod, they departed into*

their own country another way. And when they were departed, behold, the angel of the Lord appeareth to Joseph in a dream, saying, Arise, and take the young child and his mother, and flee into Egypt, and be thou there until I bring thee word: for Herod will seek the young child to destroy him. When he arose, he took the young child and his mother by night, and departed into Egypt: And was there until the death of Herod: that it might be fulfilled which was spoken of the Lord by the prophet, saying, Out of Egypt have I called my son. Then Harold, when he saw that he was mocked of the wise men, was exceeding wroth, and sent forth, and slew all the children that were in Bethlehem, and in all the costs thereof, from two years old and under, according to the time which he had diligently inquired of the wise men. Then was fulfilled that which was spoken by Jeremy the prophet, saying, In Rama was there a voice heard, lamentation, and weeping, and great mourning, Rachel weeping for her children, and would not be comforted, because they are not.

Matt. 2:12-18.

The born King survived and could not be killed by the conspiracy of Herod. So He was taken to Egypt and brought back again to the land of Israel by angelic ministration according to prophecy.

> *But when Herod was dead, behold, an angel of the Lord appeareth in a dream to Joseph in Egypt, Saying, Arise, and take the young child and his mother, and go into the land of Israel: for they are dead which sought the young child's life. And he arose, and took the young child and his mother, and came into the land of Israel.*
>
> *Matt. 2:19-21.*

So Herod who wanted the born King dead, died while the born King liveth!

Glory to the New Born King!!

Chapter Four

GLAD TIDINGS!

The birth of the new born King brought joy to the world and good news to humanity. It's the birth of the long awaited Saviour of the world. So it's good news at all time that He would be born.

Glad Tidings by the Prophets of Old

Ever before His birth there were glad tidings concerning Him by the prophets of old: that a King and a Saviour would be born that will bring salvation to the world.

> *For unto us a child is born, unto us a son is given: and the government shall be upon his shoulder: and his name shall be called Wonderful, Counsellor, The mighty God, The everlasting Father, The Prince of Peace. Of the increase of his government and peace there shall be no end, upon the throne of David, and upon his kingdom, to order it, and to establish it with judgment and with justice from henceforth even*

forever. The zeal of the LORD of hosts will perform this.

Isaiah 9:6-7.

And it shall be said in that day, Lo, this is our God; we have waited for him, and he will save us: this is the LORD; we have waited for him, we will be glad and rejoice in his salvation.

Isaiah 25:9.

But thou, Bethlehem Ephratah, though thou be little among the thousands of Judah, yet out of thee shall he come forth unto me that is to be ruler in Israel; whose goings forth have been from of old, from everlasting.

Micah 5:2.

So the prophets of old declared glad tidings of His birth to humanity before His birth.

Glad Tidings by Angels and the Host of Heaven

There were also glad tidings told by the angels before the birth, and at the birth of the new born King. Before His conception and during His conception Angels were sent to declare glad tidings of Him that is to be born King!

> *And in the sixth month the angel Gabriel was sent from God unto a city of Galilee, named Nazareth, to a virgin espoused to a man whose name was Joseph, of the house of David; and the virgin's name was Mary. And the angel came in unto her, and said, Hail, thou that art highly favoured, the Lord is with thee: blessed art thou among women. And when she saw him, she was troubled at his saying, and cast in her mind what manner of salutation this should be. And the angel said unto her, Fear not, Mary: for thou hast found favour with God. And, behold, thou shalt conceive in thy womb, and bring forth a son, and shalt call his name JESUS. He shall be great, and shall be called the Son of the Highest: and the Lord God shall give unto him the throne of his father David: And he shall reign over the house of Jacob forever; and of his kingdom there*

shall be no end. Then said Mary unto the angel, How shall this be, seeing I know not a man? And the angel answered and said unto her, The Holy Ghost shall come upon thee, and the power of the Highest shall overshadow thee: therefore also that holy thing which shall be born of thee shall be called the Son of God.

Luke 1:26-35.

Now the birth of Jesus Christ was on this wise: When as his mother Mary was espoused to Joseph, before they came together, she was found with child of the Holy Ghost. Then Joseph her husband, being a just man, and not willing to make her a publick example, was minded to put her away privily. But while he thought on these things, behold, the angel of the Lord appeared unto him in a dream, saying, Joseph, thou son of David, fear not to take unto thee Mary thy wife: for that which is conceived in her is of the Holy Ghost. And she shall bring forth a son, and thou shalt call his name JESUS: for he shall save his people from their sins. Now all this was done, that it might be fulfilled which was spoken of the Lord by the prophet, saying, Behold, a virgin shall be with child, and shall bring forth a son, and they shall call his name Emmanuel, which being interpreted is, God with us. Then Joseph being raised from sleep did as the angel of the Lord had bidden him, and took unto him his wife: And knew her not till she had brought forth her firstborn son: and he called his name JESUS.

Matt. 1:18-25.

Again at His birth, it wasn't the angel alone that declared the good tidings, the Bible recorded that the host of heaven also celebrated in declaring the great tidings of His birth.

And she brought forth her firstborn son, and wrapped him in swaddling clothes, and laid him in a manger; because there was no room for them in the inn. And there were in the same country shepherds abiding in the field, keeping watch over their flock by night. And, lo, the angel of the Lord came upon them, and the glory of the Lord shone round about them: and they were sore afraid. And the angel said unto them, Fear not: for, behold, I bring you good tidings of great joy, which shall be to all people. For unto you is born this day in the city of David a Saviour, which is Christ the

> *Lord. And this shall be a sign unto you; Ye shall find the babe wrapped in swaddling clothes, lying in a manger. And suddenly there was with the angel a multitude of the heavenly host praising God, and saying. Glory to God in the highest, and on earth peace, good will toward men.*
>
> *Luke 2:7-14.*

Glad Tidings by New Testament Prophets

It was also glad tidings from the New Testament prophets who set their eyes on Him when He was born.

> *And, behold, there was a man in Jerusalem, whose name was Simeon; and the same man was just and devout, waiting for the consolation of Israel: and the Holy Ghost was upon him. And it was revealed unto him by the Holy Ghost, that he should not see death, before he had seen the Lord's Christ. And he came by the Spirit into the temple: and when the parents brought in the child Jesus, to do for him after the custom of the law, Then took he him up in his arms, and blessed God, and said, Lord, now lettest thou thy servant depart in peace, according to thy word: For*

mine eyes have seen thy salvation, Which thou hast prepared before the face of all people; A light to lighten the Gentiles, and the glory of thy people Israel. And there was one Anna, a prophetess, the daughter of Phanuel, of the tribe of Aser: she was of a great age, and had lived with an husband seven years from her virginity; And she {was} a widow of about fourscore and four years, which departed not from the temple, but served God with fastings and prayers night and day. And she coming in that instant gave thanks likewise unto the Lord, and spake of him to all them that looked for redemption in Jerusalem.
Luke 2:25-32, 36-38.

The shepherds also declared abroad good tidings of Him to others as they told by the angel.

And it came to pass, as the angels were gone away from them into heaven, the shepherds said one to another, Let us now go even unto Bethlehem, and see this thing which is come to pass, which the Lord hath made known unto us. And they came with haste, and found Mary, and Joseph, and the babe lying in a

> *manger. And when they had seen it, they made known abroad the saying which was told them concerning this child. And all they that heard it wondered at those things which were told them by the shepherds.*
> *Luke 2:15-18.*

So the birth of the new born King is so relevant that it brought glad tidings from the Old Testament to the New Testament both to celestial beings in heaven and terrestrial beings on earth.

Joy to the World

Joy to the world the Saviour is born. His birth brought to the world salvation, redemption, and forgiveness of sins, justification, righteousness, reconciliation, adoption and eternal life to humanity.

> *And she shall bring forth a son, and thou shalt call his name JESUS: for he shall save his people from their sins.*
> *Matt. 1:21*

> *And the angel said unto them, Fear not: for, behold, I bring you good tidings of great joy, which shall be to all people. For unto you is born this day in the city of David a Saviour, which is Christ the Lord.*
> *Glory to God in the highest, and on earth peace, good will toward men.*
> *Luke 2:10-11, 14.*

Salvation brought to humanity by the new born King brought joy to the world which makes for celebration of the King! Our celebration is to acknowledge the birth of an eternal King born on earth. So if angels and the host of heaven celebrated at His birth and wise men came from afar in awe of Him to worship Him that is born a reigning King, then we must celebrate!

Let's celebrate the KING!! King of kings and Lord of lords, Glory to the New Born King: The King Eternal! All Hail King Jesus!! Amen!

With the understanding of the True Story of Christmas therefore, in our celebration of the birth of the new born

King; we must celebrate with understanding knowing the reason for which the King was born. He was born to take away our sins, and for us to get it right with the Father again.

If you haven't been born again or you're yet to get it right with the Father, then it's time for you to become born again as you receive the Lord Jesus into your life as, please say this prayer:

Lord Jesus I come to you today for the forgiveness of my sins, I believe you came to this world to save me and to die for me to have eternal life, I confess my sins today, please forgive me and have mercy on me. I believe in my heart that you're the Son of God, and I receive the Lord Jesus Christ into my life today as my Lord and Saviour. Thank you Lord for saving me in Jesus name! Amen!

Merry Christmas!!

God bless you.

Thanks for reading; we'll appreciate your positive reviews.

Other books by the Author include:

HOLY SPIRIT; GOD IN US (VOLUMES 1, 2 and 3).

And the complete volume of the book "HOLY SPIRIT; GOD IN US" only available in Hard Copy.

Contact Author @

Senior Pastor: Seed of Righteousness Kingdom Ministry.

Akure, Ondo State Nigeria.

Email: oliba139@gmail.com

Call/ WhatsApp: +234(0)8133339209.

www.ingramcontent.com/pod-product-compliance
Lightning Source LLC
LaVergne TN
LVHW010124170826
845678LV00012B/2579

* 9 7 9 8 3 6 6 4 1 4 1 7 3 *